96-4

en BV 2000

sion 2005

ndia by Roli Books in arrangement with Roli & Janssen BV
r Kailash II (Market), New Delhi-110 048, India
1) 29210886, 29212782, 29212271; Fax: ++91 (11) 29217185
@vsnl.com; Website: rolibooks.com

esign: Inkspot

ved and designed: Roli CAD Centre

er photographs: R. Krishnamurthy

inted and bound in Singapore

ISBN: 81-7436-0

© Roli & Janss
Second impre
Published in
M-75, Grea
Ph: ++91
Email: rol

Cover d

Conc

Oth

P

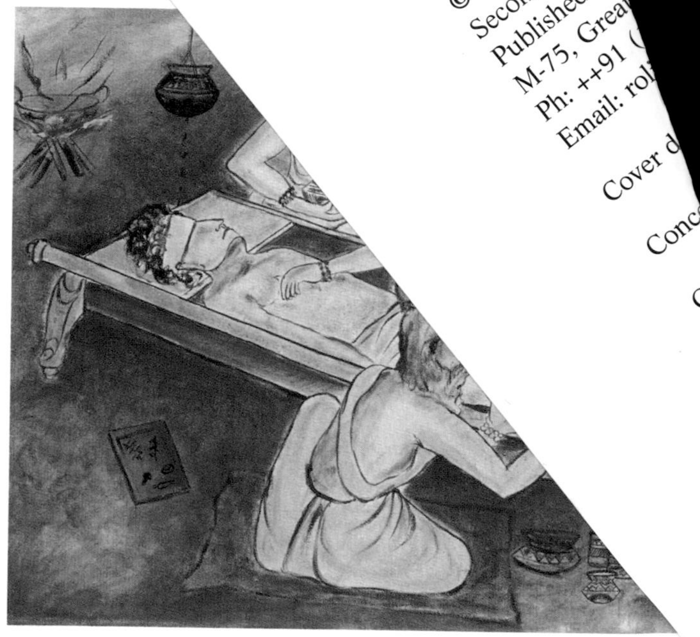

AYURVEDIC HE
MASSAG

# Ayurvedic Herbal
# MASSAGE

Text:
## Gita Ramesh

Photographs:
## Amit Pasricha

**Lustre Press**
**Roli Books**

# CONTENTS

# FOREWORD

꙳

In India the human body is equated to a temple in which the *Atma* resides and is the presiding deity. Therefore, it is enjoined upon every human being to look after the body, to nourish it, cherish and love it so that the body can, not only perform all the natural functions, but also be an instrument of greater purpose. There is a Sanskrit saying which translates as: 'The body indeed is the perfect instrument for achieving Enlightenment.'

As a classical dancer in India, I have been trained from early childhood to exercise regularly and to look after my body in every season with the appropriate means available in the form of herbs, oils, food, fruits and water. The value of a healthy body is once again appreciated in this time of galloping technological advances, which is why the underpinning of art and aesthetics in India have laid emphasis on massage. Among the five important observances, one is oil massage which should be taken every day with different kinds of oils for different seasons. Having followed this principle in my life, although not as regularly as I would have wished, the benefits are there for all to see because even in my late 50s, I am dancing with full vigour and energy, travelling, teaching and doing a hundred other things with fluent facility. As the pores of the body drink up the oil, the message of suppleness and strength passes through the body, making it glow with health and tone. Not only do I feel invigorated but also light and supple in my work which is dancing. I recommend sustained oil massages using appropriate care and material, to everybody who dreams of living a healthy and happy life.

**Sonal Mansingh**

# AYURVEDA—THE SCIENCE OF LIFE

Ayurveda—the 'Science of Life'—is one of the oldest, scientific medicinal systems in the world. The pride of India, its practice dates back to the dawn of civilisation. This age-old medical science is still pursued and practised by many people, particularly the people of Kerala—the southernmost coastal state of India. Ayurveda has two main objectives: first, to help in maintaining good health; and second, to care for the ill and restore their health. Its therapeutic approach guides man towards a lifestyle which incorporates eating wholesome food and getting a restful sleep. These result in good health and a long life.

Ayurveda takes a holistic view of health. It maintains that man, who is a part of the universe, is composed of the same elements as nature—that is, fire, earth, air, water and ether. The *Tridosha* (three elements theory) is the basis of Ayurveda. The *Tridoshas* comprise *vata* (air), *pitta* (fire) and *kapha* (water). *Vata* is considered to be present below the navel—in the urinary bladder, pelvic region, intestines, legs, thighs and bones . . . *Pitta* is present between the heart and the navel—in the navel itself, the stomach, blood, plasma, skin . . . *Kapha* is positioned in the chest, throat, head, joints, nose . . . . *Vata* stands for 'destruction', *pitta* for 'maintenance', and *kapha* for 'growth'. The *Tridoshas* in their balanced state keep the body fit and strong. When the balance gets disturbed (increases or decreases), this leads to several ailments.

When there is a proper balance of *Vata* in the body, there is a smoothness in breathing and body movements, a quickness in understanding, smooth excretion of waste materials in the body, keen eyesight and listening power. When *Vata* is aggravated, there is a lassitude in the limbs, tanning of the skin, shivering, gastric formation, constipation, sleeplessness, weakness in the body organs, giddiness and uncontrolled speech. A decrease of *Vata* in the body results in weakness, lethargy, stiffness in the body, paleness, breathing trouble and coughing, thereby making it difficult to work.

A balance of *Pitta* leads to a good appetite and proper digestion, body warmth, good eye-sight, sharp memory, wisdom, courage and a glowing and soft skin. An aggravation of *Pitta* results in pale eyes, skin, stool and urine and an increase in appetite. The body experiences a burning sensation and sleep does not come easily. On the other hand, a decrease in *Pitta* reduces the rate of digestion; the skin loses vigour and vitality and there is shivering in the body.

A proper balance of *Kapha* keeps the joints strong and maintains the desired hardness and softness in the body. If the presence of *Kapha* is aggravated, digestion becomes sluggish and the body feels stiff and lethargic. There is an excessive flow of saliva from the mouth, a coldness in the joints, breathing trouble, coughing and a sleepy feeling.

In other medical systems, any imbalance in the body is brought to order with the internal and external use of natural agents, in the form of medicines or other therapies. In Ayurveda, physical well-being is considered only a part of total health; mental and spiritual health constitute the rest. Ayurveda—with its 'Tridoshas' theory—treats the body, mind and soul.

All the therapies in Ayurveda improve general health by removing the toxins from the body and increasing its immunity. They do not simply fight a disease but rejuvenate the body. External treatments and massages play a major role in the maintenance of good health and in curative therapy. *Panchakarma*—the complete Ayurvedic health programme—promotes fitness through massages with medicated herbal oils. Various medicated oils, important constituents in massage therapies, are made with different combinations of herbs. They are processed to suit the constitution and complaint of each individual. Massage with these oils builds stamina and energy, and protects the body from illnesses.

Massage exercises the whole body, tones up the muscles, improves blood circulation, repairs worn-out tissues, removes toxins and knocks off fat. In women, massage improves the complexion (it is the first step towards a youthful and glowing skin) and body posture, and nourishment of the inner self.

Besides the massages which promote general good health and tone up the muscles, there are special massages for treating ailments. These massages have been noticeably successful in treating rheumatism, arthritis, lumbago, hypertension, spondylitis, slipped disk, paralysis, palsy, migraine, nervous debility, sinusitis, chronic cold, obesity and depression. These treatments focus on the root cause rather than the symptoms. Ayurvedic massages are the only proven and trusted remedies for such ailments.

While undergoing these therapies, a positive attitude is essential for proper results. Regular massages protect the body from falling prey to ailments, arrest premature aging and tone up the skin. They relieve stress and help to promote a long and healthy life. ∎

# ABHYANGAM—FULL BODY MASSAGE

A healthy glowing skin, an agile body and a complete sense of well-being is everybody's dream. In these days of hectic lifestyles, with everyday tensions in a pollution-ridden urban life increasing, there is a ray of hope—a distinct possibility of bubbling with vigour and vitality. For this we must look to our ancient system of healthy living—Ayurveda.

Ayurvedic massage has a hypnotic effect on the body and mind; it is deeply relaxing and boosts the body's circulation. When the body and mind are both at peace, one's face reflects the inner calm. Moreover, rubbing the body with medicated herbal oils works as a tonic and increases one's energy.

Much of what we consider to be everyday routine and do mechanically—such as rubbing oil on the whole body and taking a warm bath—are, in fact, techniques of health care. These are the very routines preached by Ayurveda. Ayurveda advises the practice of daily massage of the body with oil. This is the best way of preserving youthfulness; massaging the whole body has a greater impact: it relaxes, cleanses and creates a harmony between the mind and the body.

The massage is performed by two Ayurvedic therapists working in perfect synchrony. It is followed by a steam bath which helps the oils to penetrate thoroughly, cleanse the body and remove the toxins lodged deep within the tissues. The steam bath is followed by a warm shower. The shower removes all the dirt and revitalises the body. Bathing every day not only removes dirt, but also revitalises the body, stimulates appetite, prevents itching and chases lethargy away. If we do not take time out for these seemingly small things, we will diminish the quality of our lives. Massages are recommended for children too. They assist in growth and strengthen the immune system.

Oil is needed in a massage for the masseur's strokes to be smooth and flowing. The masseur's hands must be able to slide against the surface of the skin without friction. Each part of the hand is employed in the massage—the heel, thumb, palm and fingers. Only warm oils should be used.

Massage helps in loosening muscular tension, opens up the pores of the skin and improves its tonal quality. During a massage, the body is rubbed vigorously to allow the oil to be absorbed; the pressure being firm, yet not uncomfortable. Different types of oils are used for the head, face and the body.

Ayurvedic massages are done with herbal oils only. Various herbs are used in the preparation of oils; some are listed on pp. 72-79. The oils to be used are selected depending on the body type.

I

*The first part of Abhyangam or Full Body Massage is done with the subject sitting upright.*

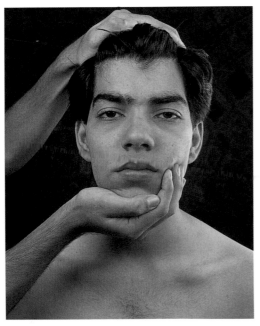

**1** ▲

## Head

The subject sits on the *droni* (specially carved wooden bed), with legs stretched out and arms on the side. The room in which the massage takes place should be comfortably warm. Two masseurs stand on either side of the subject undergoing the massage. (The masseurs/masseuses have to be highly knowledgeable and must enjoy doing the massage).

**1.** Pour a generous quantity of warm oil into the palm. Slowly pour the oil on the head of the subject who is sitting upright on the *droni*. With the palm of the left hand kept flat on the subject's head and the other hand cupping the chin firmly, rub the palm on the soft spot of the head (or crown) vigorously so that the maximum oil is absorbed by the head. The oil not only cools and relaxes the subject but has a lot of curative values and acts as a healing medicine. ■

## Face and Neck

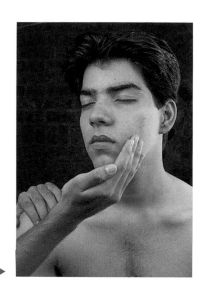

**1 ▶**

1. Apply oil on the subject's face with the finger tips and rub all over gently.

2. Dip the fingers into the bowl of body oil. Rub both hands with the oil thoroughly. First spread the oil over the neck area, allowing the surface of the muscles to relax. Holding the arm with the left hand, rub the nape of the neck downwards with the palm and fingers. Do these strokes very gently. Before massaging, spread each area with warm oil. Never pour directly over the body. ■

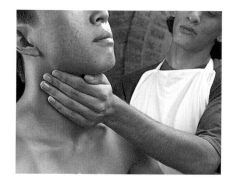

**2 ▲**

---

## Back

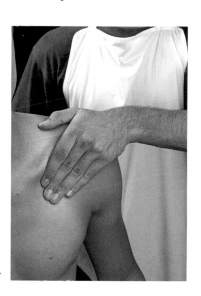

**1 ▶**

1. Circle the shoulder with the fingers and heel of the hand and massage. Circling helps to release and relax the muscles.

2. Then apply oil on both the shoulders with the palms flat and fingers together. With the fingers resting on the shoulders and pointing downwards towards the chest, massage the shoulders in an outward direction, giving a push to the shoulders.

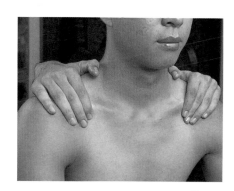

**2 ▲**

3. Divide the back into two portions (each masseur concentrating on his assigned

**4 ▼**

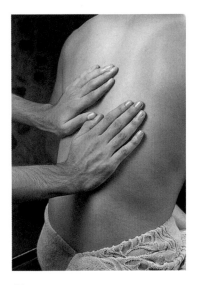

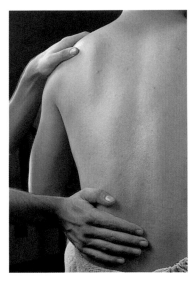

**3 ▲**

portion). Apply warm medicated oil all over the back with the finger tips.

Massage the back with the hands placed flat, one beside the other. From the top of the shoulder downwards, massage vigorously, exerting pressure with the palm while going downwards till the buttocks. The subject sits erect throughout this step of massage and the whole back is massaged, emphasising on the vertebral column. The posture is very important.

The back is the largest and the most important area. While massaging it, the subject feels very comfortable and is able to relax easily as the back contains many nerves and nerve endings. Any massage done on the back has a direct and profound effect on the subject's body.

**4.** With one hand on the shoulder rub in and out sideways in a circular motion. Circling the hip, place the heel of your hands on the curve just above the hip. Slowly circle away, pressing in for the oil to penetrate even more. Pressing also relaxes the muscles over the specific area.

**5.** Applying steady pressure, move your flat palm in circular motion over the sacrum or the last vertebrate. ■

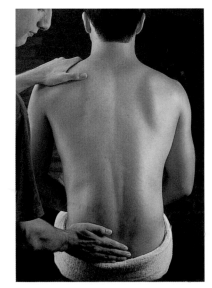

**5 ▲**

# Chest

**1.** Using the palm and fingers in a circular motion, massage over the entire front of the body, moving upwards and outwards from the body mid-line. Glide your palm smoothly out towards the shoulder.

**2.** Moving your hand on the neck in a circular motion, slide down with a firm and steady movement to give the muscles a good stretch. Repeat this in a flowing sequence. These 'ease' strokes release tension from the joints such as the neck, shoulders and pelvis. ∎

# Legs and Feet

**1.** The **thigh** is an area where fats and toxins collect easily and get trapped due to sluggish circulation. This is mostly due to a sedentary lifestyle. Most problems relating to the thighs are due to accumulation of cellulite, the skin being dry, and flabby thighs. Apply oil on the thigh. Massage the thigh kneading and squeezing with the palm and thumb to ease tense muscles and tone up the sluggish system. Massage the inner surface of the thigh with your palm and fingers. The fat deposits on the thighs can be broken down by improved circulation and eliminated.

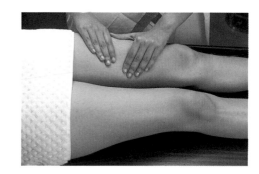

**2.** Next do a synchronised massage of the legs. Using both hands with fingers pointing inwards and thumbs, one on top of the other, massage the outer surface of the leg, starting from the hip and going down to the toes,

1 ▲

**3** ▼

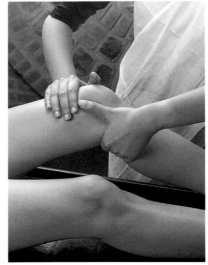

**2** ▲

applying pressure as you go downwards. After reaching the toes, proceed upwards again, using very little pressure as you go upwards.

**3.** Massage the inner surface of the legs with your palm and fingers.

**4.** Tackle the **knees** next. With your palm, massage clockwise around the whole knee in a circular motion. Exerting pressure, massage the top of the knees.

With four fingers below the knee and the thumb on the top of the knee, keep stroking the inner region of the knee from side to side; this releases tension. Extra care should be taken to massage below the knees.

**5.** The **calves** need to be toned regularly. With one hand massage the calf vigorously, starting from the top and going downwards.

**6.** Cupping the **ankle** with the fingers and the thumb, rub the oil in a circular manner vigorously into the whole ankle joint, emphasising the areas around the bones on the inner and outer side of the ankle.

**4** ▲

**5** ▼

**7.** Next move down to the **feet.** Using the thumb and fingers, press both thumbs over the entire surface of the foot, one spot at a time, while supporting the foot with the other fingers. This normally relaxes the tension in the area.

Massage the top and sole of the foot simultaneously by allowing the heel to rest on the *droni* and rubbing the top and sole with both the palms.

**8.** Using oil liberally cup the heel with your palms and massage in a rubbing action from left to right. Foot massage prevents and cures dryness, numbness, roughness, fatigue and cracking of the heels. It gives you strength while walking and running.

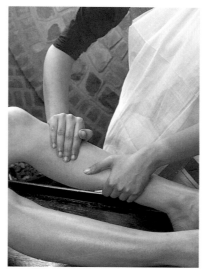

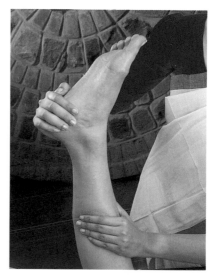

**8** ▲

**9.** Stretch each toe from the big toe to the little toe, using a good quantity of oil. With one hand holding the heal firmly, press all fingers of the other hand at the back of the toes, exerting pressure forwards (see Fig. 7). ■

**7** ▲

*Note: The entire leg from hip to toe is massaged with both hands kept flat one beside the other and applying steady pressure in a smooth flowing movements. This makes for a synchronised massage.*

# II

## The second part of Abhyangam is done with the subject lying on his back

**1.** Placing your palms on the subject's shoulders, with the thumbs in front and four fingers at the back, massage the shoulder well.

Using sideway movements massage the back of the neck.

**2.** Make the subject rest his arm on the *droni*. Placing both the palms on the arm, massage from the top of the shoulder to the tips of the fingers.

2 ▼

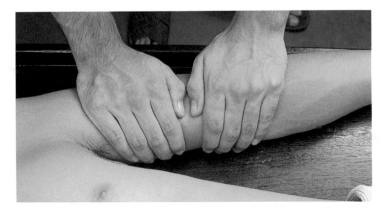

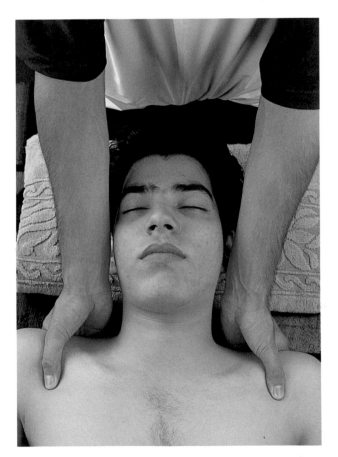

1 ▲

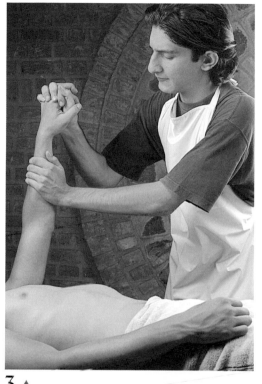

**3.** Interlocking the fingers of the subject with your own, lift the arm at a right angle and massage the inner arms.

**4.** Lower the hand and, with the heel of the hand, rub the palm and pull each finger. Stroke the back of the hand with the palms in a circular motion and then down each finger, pulling each finger with three fingers. Rub the palm and smoothen it out.

**5.** Keeping your fingers interlocked with those of the subjects, lift the latter's arm straight upwards. Massage the arm pit with the whole hand. First concentrate on one side of the arm—that is, the inner side of the arm and then, concentrate on the outer side of the arm. Thus work along the natural curves and shapes of the muscles. This motion can also be done vigorously with the arms (almost) being pulled. The stretching affects the fibrous tissues around the joints and reduces muscle tension, giving a sense of expansion.

3 ▲

4 ▼

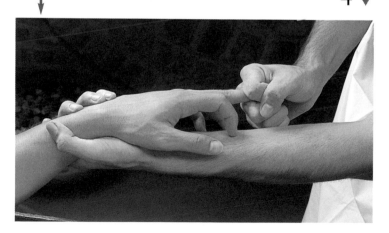

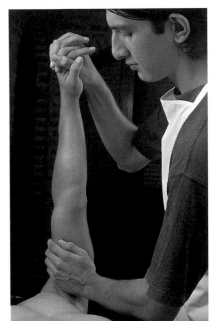

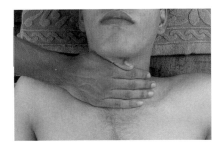

**6.** Massage the front of the neck from left to right with the palm and all fingers flat.

**7.** Placing both palms flat on the abdomen, massage the lower abdomen in a circular manner from left to right.

Next, massage the upper abdomen. Position both hands over the abdomen, one beside the other. (Each masseur's hands should be on either side of the navel). Slowly begin circling in a clockwise direction, hands flat against the body. As you circle, lift your hands alternatively so that the hands cross and the massage goes on in a continuous process. Always circle gently and take care not to press deep.

**8.** Massage the back of the thighs and knees, the inner and outer portions of the legs, the ankles and top and sole of the feet.

Lift and bend the subject's knee, pushing the heel backwards so that it touches the buttocks. Repeat 3-4 times to relax the knee joint. ■

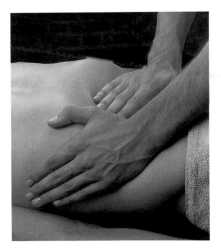

# III

*The third part of Abhyangam is carried out with the subject lying on the stomach*

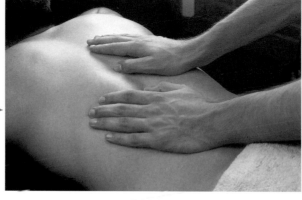

**1** ▼

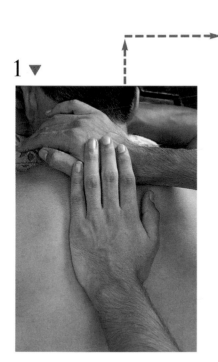

While in this position a lot of emphasis is given to the spinal column. The back massage is divided into four stages:

**1.** Massage the area just below the neck vigorously. Proceed downwards towards the sacrum, massaging with flat palms.

**2.** Massage the sacrum in a circular manner with the palms and fingers.

**2** ▼

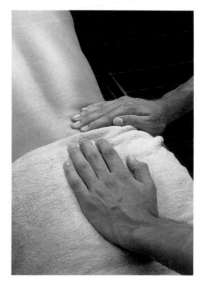

**3.** Move the palms in a circular manner over the buttocks. Start from the upper part and move downwards, keeping the circular motion going.

**4.** Now concentrate on the back of the leg. Massage from the hip to the heel with both hands vigorously. Spend a little extra time on the inner portion of the knees, using greater concentration as you do so.

**5.** Bend the lower part of the leg towards the back till the heel touches the buttocks. Then massage the lower leg in this position.

◀ 3

5 ▼

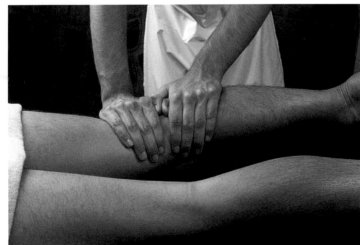

4 ▲

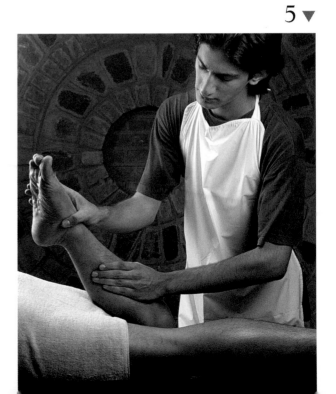

The *Abhyangam* takes about 45 minutes. After the massage, take the subject for a steam bath. The steam bath should last for three minutes.

Since the steam opens up the pores in the body, the toxins are removed. The oil also penetrates deepcr into the tissues, thus improving the circulation of the blood and rejuvenating the body.

After the massage remove the oil by using various herbal powders. Make the herbal powder into a paste with the required quantity of water and rub all over the body—first, over the trunk, then on the arms, fingers, legs, toes, neck, face and ears. Pay special attention to the hard skin on the elbows, knees, soles and heels. Rubbing these areas with the herbal powders not only removes the oils—it also has a softening effect.

The subject should then take a bath or a shower, at the end of which, his skin will feel very soft and supple. ∎

*Below left: The steam chamber is the traditional one used for Ayurvedic massages. An ordinary steam bath is the modern-day equivalent of the same.*

*Below: Herbal powder rubbed on the body after the massage, has a soothing effect.*

# BASIC TECHNIQUES *for Abhyangam*

▼ EFFLEURAGE is the most basic stroke in *Abhyangam*. It is a circular inward-stroking movement made with the palm of the hand. The same technique is also used in self-massage. Effleurage is done mainly to spread oil over the whole body. The strokes are smooth and flowing and are applied with a steady pressure.

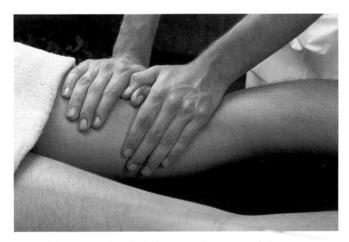 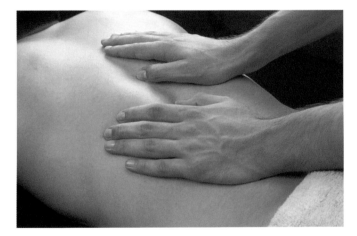

*Note: Move your hands in long strokes, up and down.*

They are also very gentle and relaxing. When starting a massage over any area, it is always effleuraged with warm medicated herbal oils. The oil is never poured directly over the body. Large sweeping strokes are used to cover the entire area. Not only are they very soothing, they also help in the body circulation. Effleurage can be done on the legs, arms, back, lower back and hips.

▶ KNEADING is a pummeling action done with the entire hand. The fleshy areas of the body benefit from kneading, which eases tense muscles and tones up a sluggish sytem. The area which is being attended to must be thoroughly oiled so that no pain is felt. Kneading is of great use on the arms, legs, calves and thigh region where fatty deposits are trapped. It helps in breaking down these deposits, increasing the blood circulation and eliminating toxins, which can cause stiffness and pain.

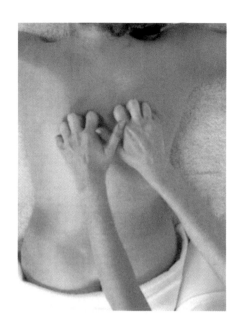

◀ PRESSING is used to release the muscles over a specific and usually small area where kneading is not possible. It is usually done with the thumb, the finger tips or with the heel of the hand. Pressing is effective on the forehead, the palm, soles of the feet, the spine, shoulders and the inner region of the knees.

The movement is precise and applied by deeply stroking over a particularly tight area of muscle such as the side of the spinal chord. This eases tension around the vertebrae. The pressure should be applied gently and should feel comfortable to the receiver.

Using the heel pressure is a way of increasing pressure over large areas of muscles. When applied on a specific area, like the hips, under the feet or on the shoulders, it helps in deeper penetration.

▼ PULLING is best used on the toes and fingers. There are many pressure points on the hands and feet and they respond very well when they are pressed and pulled.

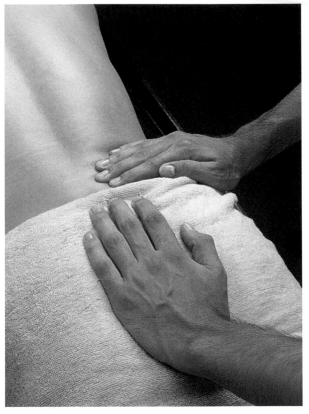

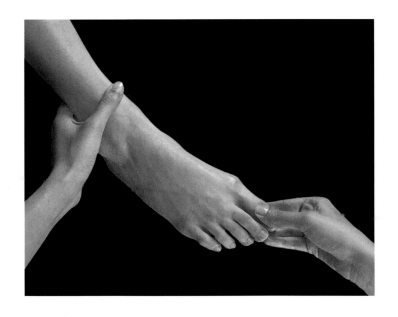

▲ CIRCLING is done over the soft rather than the thick areas of the muscles. Used to release or gently diffuse the effect of kneading, it is ideal for the wrist joints. Done with the thumbs or the flat of the hand, it is also an effective method of massage on the sacrum, abdomen, shoulders, hips, neck, knees and ankles.

# Head

The head is the centre of the whole nervous system. Stress, strain and other problems concerning the upper region of the body have a direct impact on the growth and condition of the hair. Poor circulation of the scalp is the root cause of many hair problems. The scalp has to be nourished very well. If neglected, it tends to be scaly, itchy and smelly due to the layers of the dead cells and the bacteria breeding on the scalp. The best way to keep the scalp clean and healthy is to massage it regularly. The condition of the hair depends on the quality of the nutrients that are taken and the general state of health. The head massage also has a positive effect on the brain and nervous system, improving concentration and intelligence. A special hair oil is used for the head massage. The oil is absorbed into the roots of the brain which, in turn, are connected to the nerve fibres. The oil strengthens the hair and removes dryness, prevents loss of hair and premature baldness. A head massage should be done every day before a shower in the morning.

**1.** Part the hair in the centre and pour in a sufficient quantity of oil in the centre of the head in the soft spot, or the fontanelle point, and rub it in with the palm.

1 ▼

**2** ▼

**2.** Dip the fingers into the oil again and with the finger tips, massage the side of the head, tilting the head on one side. Do this on the left side first and then on the right side.

**3** ▼

**3.** Bend the head down and pour some oil on the base of the skull. Rub the oil in vigorously with the fingers. This action stimulates the body. In this manner, massage the entire scalp upwards.

**4.** The scalp needs regular nourishing and blood circulation should be good. The medicated herbal oil not only improves circulation but strengthens the follicles. The massage increases the blood supply around the hair follicles, thus providing nourishment and a healthy sheen to the hair.

Poor blood circulation is the cause of various problems. Nourishing your hair with a good medicated oil and massaging it regularly keeps the follicles active, strengthens the hair, increases the blood supply to the head and removes tension.

4 ▶

5 ▶

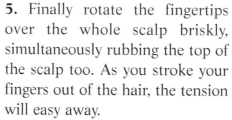

**5.** Finally rotate the fingertips over the whole scalp briskly, simultaneously rubbing the top of the scalp too. As you stroke your fingers out of the hair, the tension will easy away.

Wash the hair with water at room temperature. Washing the hair with hot water leads to hair loss and premature greying, and is bad for the eyes. As a good quantity of oil is used, a shampoo will be required to wash the oil off from the hair. Take any good herbal powder shampoo and make it into a paste. Rub it into the hair with your fingertips, moving from the hairline towards the centre. Then wash it off with plenty of water. If the oil does not come off in the first wash, apply the shampoo once again. The hair should be washed every day, especially if the subject is suffering from dandruff or psoriasis. ■

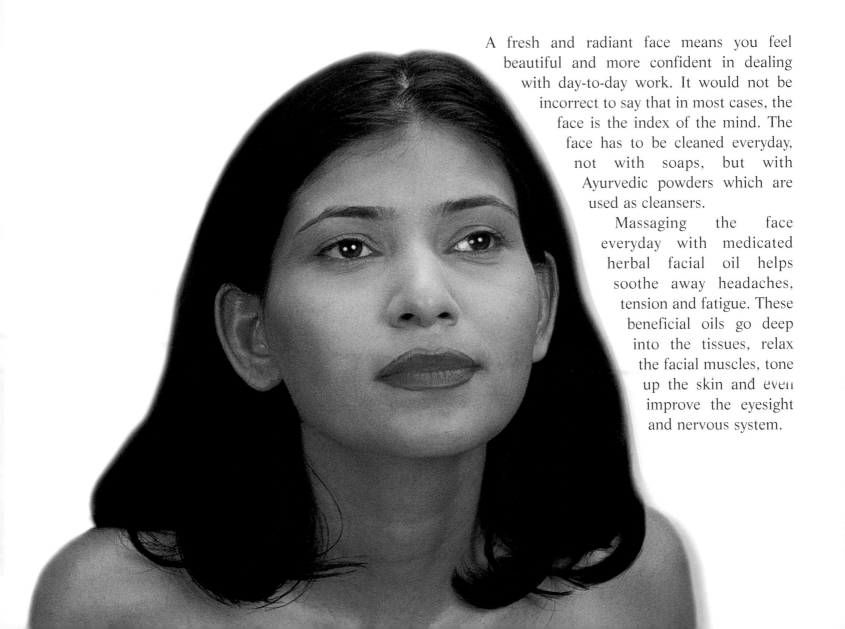

# Face

A fresh and radiant face means you feel beautiful and more confident in dealing with day-to-day work. It would not be incorrect to say that in most cases, the face is the index of the mind. The face has to be cleaned everyday, not with soaps, but with Ayurvedic powders which are used as cleansers.

Massaging the face everyday with medicated herbal facial oil helps soothe away headaches, tension and fatigue. These beneficial oils go deep into the tissues, relax the facial muscles, tone up the skin and even improve the eyesight and nervous system.

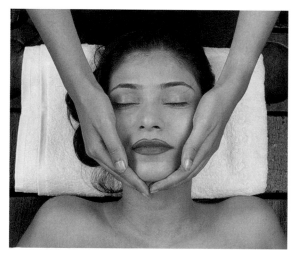

◄ **1**

**1.** With your finger tips apply oil on the chin, both cheeks and forehead. Rub both your hands with a good quantity of oil. Cupping the chin in your palms, starting from the chin region, massage upwards in a sweeping action gently to dispose of any congestion.

**2.** Position your fingers under the chin and place the thumbs on top of the chin. Keep pressing and gliding till you reach the corner of the jaw bone and apply pressure just below the ear lobes.

**2** ▼

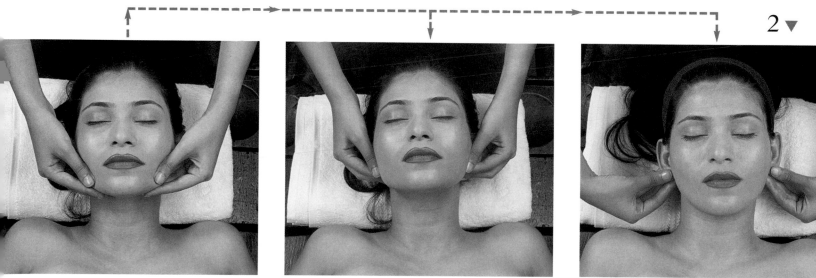

**3.** Massage the cheeks in a circular manner: this helps to remove the dead cells from the surface of the skin.

**4.** Placing your fingers on the cheeks and your thumbs on either side of the nose, move in a circular manner upwards to the mid-point between the eyebrows. In a gentle clockwise motion massage the area on the forehead just above the eyebrows and then the full forehead.

**5.** With the fingers lightly massage the forehead. There are two ways in which this can be done. Place the fingers on the cheeks (5a) and the thumbs above and between the eyebrows. Massage the forehead, moving from the centre, outwards.

Alternately, place the thumbs on either side of the temples. Placing the remaining fingers on the forehead (5b), massage outwards, pressing the temples.

6 ▲

7 ▲

**6.** With the index fingers massage just above and below the lips in a circular manner.

**7.** With your thumbs just above the eyebrows, and the index fingers just below them, massage the eyebrows from the inner to the outer corner of the eyes.

**8.** Massage the neck from left to right in a rhythmical upward manner. Use a stroking motion, with one hand following the other. ■

8 ▲

# Ears

The ear is one of the most delicate organs of the body. The auditory nerve is the thoroughfare through which signals are conveyed to the brain. An ear massage needs to be done very carefully.

2 ▲

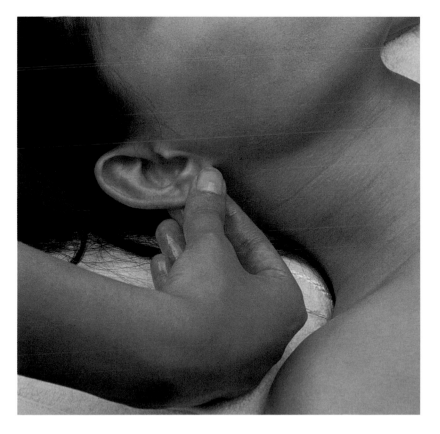

**1.** Hold the ear-lobe between the thumb and the index finger.

**2.** With a rolling and gently squeezing motion, move along the outer edge of the ear. Continue till you reach the point where the ear connects with the head. Rub the entire outer portion of the ear in the same manner, as also the outer ridge.

◄ 1

 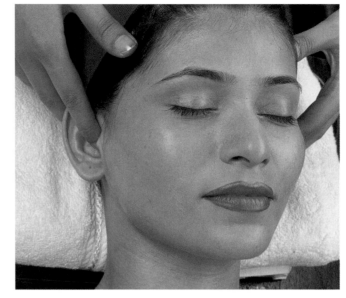

**3.** Rub the ear where it is attached to the head, starting behind the lobe and working your way up behind the ear to the point where the top portion is attached to the head.

**4.** Insert one finger gently into the inner surface of the ear. Rub gently, ensuring that the ear drum is not damaged. ∎

# Neck

The neck can feel stiff and inflexible often due to tension in the chest and shoulders. A neck massage helps to ease this tension.

Placing the hands at an angle below the skull, slide firmly down the exposed side of the neck adding pressure with the heels to stretch the muscles. Soften the pressure as your hands sweep around the shoulder joints and glide up behind the neck.

The uric acid granules deposited in these areas start breaking and get eliminated. ■

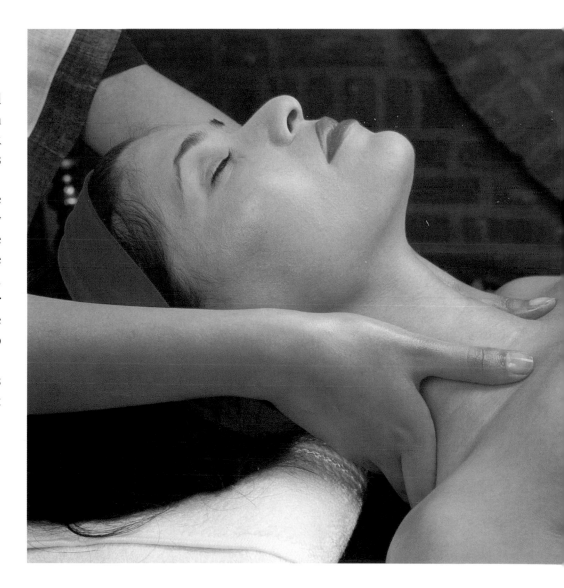

# SPECIALISED MASSAGES

Specialised massages are ayurvedic therapies which have been practised in Kerala for a long time. Known as Kerala Art, these therapies or *Swedana* are of different types and are used for various types of ailments. These procedures restore the balance of the three *doshas* and improve the power of the sensory organs.

These massage therapies are one of the important therapeutic procedures which expel the impurities in the body in chronic diseases like arthritis, rheumatism, neurological problems and other disorders. They also help in curing sciatica, polio, spondylitis, sinusitis, paralysis, migraine, insomnia, backache . . . They can increase immunity, cure diseases at the initial stages and prevent the instant intake of medicines. They also sharpen memory, reduce body fat, improve skin tone and enable peaceful sleep. Practitioners claim that they eradicate diseases permanently from the roots so that a relapse does not occur.

The massages described hereafter should be done only under the guidance of a qualified physician. The physician should be knowledgeable and experienced. The patient must have full faith in the physician while undergoing these therapies.

It is important to consider the season before deciding to take up any of these treatments. The rainy season, that is mid-July to August, is considered to be the best time or period to undergo treatments like *Dhara*, *Pizhichil* and *Navrakizhi*. This month is known as the Karkitakam in the Kerala calendar and is good for restoring the balance of the *tridoshas*.

Seasonal rules need not be followed in cases that require immediate attention, where no strict regimen is to be followed and for minor ailments. However, care has to be taken to protect patients from heat, cold and rain. If the treatment advises a strict regimen, it should be properly followed to the letter. Some of the regimen to be followed include bathing in warm water; eating at proper times and in prescribed quantities; avoiding excess reading, talking, sitting, walking; and not sleeping during the day.

The environment where the treatments are performed should also be taken into consideration. Places that have polluted air should be completely avoided.

These therapies are administered to suit an individual's physical and mental needs and they help one lead a healthy, balanced and long life.

# Pizhichil

*A special massage for rejuvenating the whole body,* Pizhichil *protects one from illness and builds up immunity.*

Usually three experienced masseurs are required for this treatment. One masseur is required for heating the oil and supplying it to the other masseurs during the treatment. (However, the photographs here show the process being conducted by one masseur.)

**1.** Make the patient sit upright and apply oil to his head and shoulders.

**2.** Then make the patient lie down. Dip the pieces of linen cloth well into the oil and squeeze the oil over the body, while massaging the body with the hands all the time. Massage very slowly without exerting much pressure, taking care to cover every part of the body. Heat the oil occasionally. The whole process takes about one hour to complete.

**3.** After the massage, wipe the body and let the patient take a bath. Take great care to wipe the head dry and apply medicated powder to the patient's body so that he does not catch a cold.

The massage procedure of *Pizhichil* is very similar to *Abhyangam.* The only difference is that the oil is poured on the body throughout the process of the therapy and very little pressure is exerted during massage.

*Pizhichil* is effective in the treatment of rheumatic diseases, blood pressure, diabetes and pain in the joints. ∎

*Note: This therapy must be performed only under the supervision of a physician.*

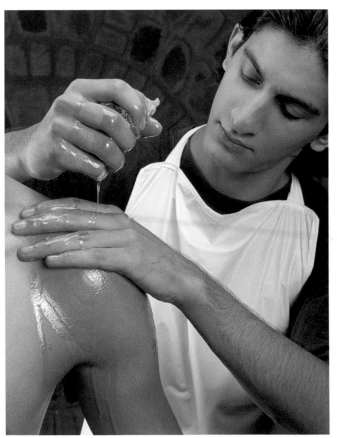

1 ▲

**6a** ▶

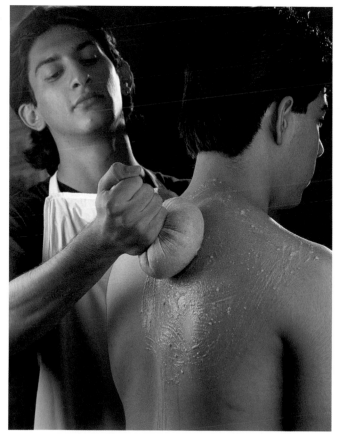

**6b** ▶

**4.** Make four equal bundles (poultices) of the rice-herbal decoction mixture and keep aside.

**5.** Apply medicated oil all over the patient's body. (The selection of oil must suit the patient's temperament and symptoms of the disease.)

**6.** Dip the bundles into a mixture comprising the

# Navrakizhi

*An effecitve therapy for treating paralysis and hemiplegia (paralysis of one side of the body).*

**1.** In two separate lots, finely cut and crush the roots of *Sida rhombifolia* in 16 times the amount of water for each lot. Cook until only one-fourth of the decoction is left and strain. Keep aside.

**2.** Separately cook one kilogram of Narva rice (grown in Kerala) in four litres of undiluted milk.

**3.** Add one lot of the herbal decoction to the rice and cook till almost dry.

second lot of herbal decoction and an equal quantity of milk (6a) and massage over the entire body (6b). The poultices should be neither too hot or too cold.

**7.** After an hour of massage, wipe the rice paste off the body.

**8.** Apply the medicated oil once again. If this course is followed through for 14 days consecutively, it is an excellent treatment for imparting lustre to the skin and nourishing the body. ■

*Note: This therapy must be performed only under the supervision of a physician.*

# Talapothichil

*An ideal treatment for falling hair, dandruff and greying. Beneficial for insomnia, low blood pressure and chronic sinusitis.*

**1.** Soak about 25 gm of *amla* (gooseberries) without seeds in 900 ml of buttermilk overnight. Only an earthen vessel should be used for soaking the *amla*.

**2.** Grind the mixture coarsely and keep aside.

5 ▲

**3.** Apply oil to the subject's head.

**4.** Tie a *varti* (roll of cloth) around the head just above the ears and eyebrows. It should be comfortably tight.

**5.** Apply the ground paste to the crown of the head first, then the frontal area, right side of the

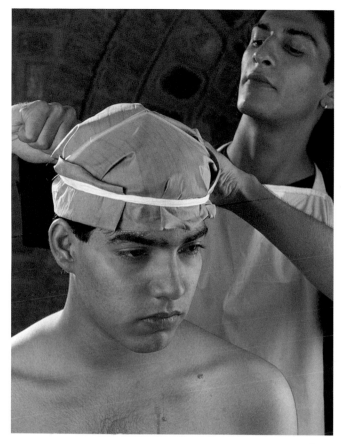

6 ▲

head, the back, and lastly, the left side. The paste applied should have a uniform thickness of three centimetres.

**6.** Cover the head with a banana leaf and leave it on for 45 minutes.

**7.** Remove the paste and wipe the head clean. ■

# Khadikizhi

*An excellent therapy for skin problems, high blood pressure and for diluting lymph nodes.*

**1.** Dry and powder an equal quantity of *vacha*, *til*, deodar, mustard and castor seeds. Make bundles of the powder and tie in pieces of muslin cloth.

**2.** Make a herbal decoction by boiling and cooking 100 gm each of sugarcane, lime, rice husk, tina rice (grown only in Kerala), wheat and lentils like green gram, horse gram and white gram in 10 litres of water.

**3.** Steam the herbal bundles in the herbal decoction and keep aside.

**4.** Apply medicated oil all over the subject's body and then massage every part of the body with the steamed bundles. ■

*Note: This therapy must only be performed under the supervision of a physician.*

1 ▶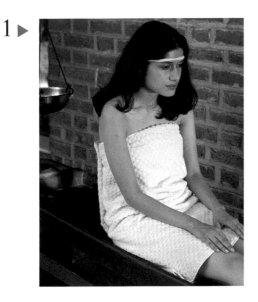

massage therapy for stress, strain and spondylitis.

The following items are required for the *Dhara* treatment:

- *Droni or dharapaati* (specially carved wooden bed).
- *Dhara Chatti* (a special vessel made of clay or metal that does not have any negative effect on any kind of liquid used in the treatment). The vessel has a hole at the base.
- Wick.

## Dhara

*The best therapy for rejuvenation of the mind and body.*

Understanding the principle behind *Dhara* therapy is very important. The massage therapy should be conducted by experienced persons only and in the presence of a physician. *Dhara* is a specialised treatment which is good for insanity, ailments related to the head and the eyes, chronic colds and sinusitis, diseases of the ear and mouth, rheumatoid arthritis, abscesses, wounds, swellings. This therapy also rejuvenates and revitalises the mind and body and diminishes the ill-effects of aging. *Dhara* is also a special

5 ▶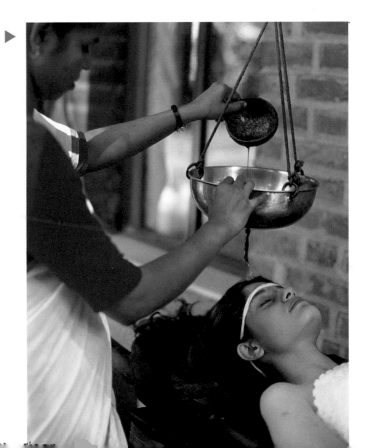

- Coconut shell.
- A roll of cloth known as *varti*, to tie around the head.
- A pillow covered with a soft cloth.

**1.** Make the patient sit on the *droni*. Take some oil in the palm of the hand and apply it on the crown of the patient's head.

**2.** Tie the *varti* around the head just above the ears and eyebrows. It should not be too tight or too loose. The knot should only be on the side of the head.

**3.** Liberally apply the medicated oil on the patient's head and body.

**4.** Make the patient comfortable in a supine position on the wooden bed. Ensure that the head and neck are not strained in any way.

**5.** Pour the oil into the *Dhara* vessel slowly, allowing the liquid to move down along the wick gradually.

**6.** Bring the vessel forward and move it to and fro from left to right slowly. Massage the scalp under the hair with the free palm at intervals.

The *Dhara* vessel should be handled with great concentration and attention so that the liquid or oil does not fall into the patient's eyes.

The flow should not break at any time during the process of the treatment. This process goes on for almost one hour. As the *Dhara* progresses, the patient's body is massaged very lightly. However it is massaged only in the front area from the shoulders to the toes (as described in the chapter on *Abhyangam*), while the patient is lying down on his back. ∎

*Note: This therapy must be performed only under the supervision of a physician.*

# SELF-MASSAGE — A KEEP-FIT PROGRAMME

Ayurveda recommends oil massages every day to keep fit and energetic and to lead a healthy life. Self-massage is almost like an exercise regime. These massages, when done with herbal oils, not only tone the skin but nourish it too. The simple steps that are required for a person to massage oneself every day are discussed here.

Soon after one rises in the morning, nature's call must be answered. The next step is mouth hygiene. Brush your teeth and clean your tongue with a scraper to clean it thoroughly. This helps the teeth to be free of bacteria and keeps the mouth fresh and clean.

Next in line is care of the eyes: they should be rinsed with cold water. Water should be splashed on the eyes for almost five minutes. Then the body should be strengthened by a massage. The massage not only exercises the body but reduces body fat, removes deep-seated deposits and dead skin. The massage should be done in a warm room. It starts with the head and is completed at the toes.

1 ▶

## Head

**1.** Warm the oil in a container. Part your hair, dab some oil in the centre of the head and give it a brisk rub.

**2.** Using both your hands keep rubbing the left side and the right side simultaneously with the palms. Pass your fingers through your hair inch by inch from the hairline to the centre of the head in a combing fashion.

3 ▼

◀ 2

**3.** When both the sides have been massaged, bend forward and apply some oil just above the nape of the neck and rub it in with the palms.

 4

**4.** Again, with your fingers keep rubbing and applying pressure from the nape to the crown. This way the whole scalp is massaged and the full length of the hair is also rubbed with the oil. This improves the blood ciculation. If your hair is long, collect it together and make a bun on the top of your head. ∎

# Face

**3** ▶

◀ **2**

**1.** Pour the oil into your left palm and with the index finger of your right hand, dip into the oil.

**2.** Apply it first on your forehead. Two to three drops on the forehead should be sufficient. After the forehead put a drop of oil on your left cheek, then on your right cheek. Lastly put a drop on your chin. Now rub both your palms together so that they are smeared with oil.

**3.** With your finger tips, make circular movements on your forehead so that the oil spreads on the entire forehead.

**4** ▼

**5** ▲

**4.** Placing the thumbs on the temples, keep massaging your forehead to and fro with the other four fingers, exerting slight pressure. This helps to release tension. Tension restricts the flow of the blood and the removal of wastes from the tissues, making the skin more prone to wrinkles.

**5.** With both the thumbs rub the nose from between the eyebrows to the tip of the nose at least five times.

**6**. Now with your thumbs below your eyebrows and index fingers above the eyebrows, massage the area from the centre outwards five times. Take care that no oil gets into the eyes.

**7**. With your fingers spread the oil on the chin. Cup the chin with the palm of your hand and massage from the chin to the ear with each palm alternately. As you end just below the ear lobes, apply pressure for a second. Do this massage on the chin five times. Hold with your thumbs and four fingers and keep gliding along the jaw line with pressure. This helps the fat that is accumulated there to disperse and gives the face a defined shape.

7 ▲

6 ▶

8 ▲          9 ▲

**8.** The cheeks are now rubbed very lightly with fingers and palms. With the left hand on the left cheek and the right hand on the right cheek, this is done for almost two minutes. The skin has a tendency to accumulate dead cells. All the dead cells that are accumulated on the surface of the skin are removed by this action and the skin is able to breathe.

**9.** Massage the ears with the thumbs and index fingers (for details, see Ear Massage). Hence by facial massage the skin gets sufficient oil and tension is released—this keeps your face radiant.     ■

# *Body*

Warm the oil for the body massage in a container. Dip your fingers into a good quantity of oil and rub both your hands together.

1 ▶

**1.** Spread the oil on the entire front part of the neck. Massage upwards from the base of the neck to the chin in a rhythmic motion, one hand following the other. Keep the head tilted slightly backwards. This prevents the neck from becoming wrinkled, any fat being deposited in the area and hence, the formation of a double chin.

**2**. Dip your fingers into the oil container and spread the oil on the back of the neck, touching the entire surface of the neck on the back and the two sides. This movement provides a soothing effect to the whole head. Next, with the left hand first, start massaging with the fingers and palm placed flat on the neck, pressing hard as if almost circling the neck. Repeat this stroke with the right hand. Do these strokes ten times each.

2 ▶

**3.** With the right hand massage the left shoulder and with the left hand, the right shoulder. First spread the oil on the left shoulder with the finger tips of your right hand. Massage, pressing and exerting pressure in a circular motion, as if almost pulling out the shoulders. Now in the same manner apply oil on the right shoulder with the left hand and massage it.

**4.** With the right hand apply oil on the outer surface of the left arm (4a) from the shoulders till the tip of the fingers (4b), palm kept flat on the arm and fingers encircling the arm. Massage from the shoulders to the tip of the fingers. As you proceed from the top of the shoulder downwards, exert pressure with the heel of the hand on the arms. Spend two minutes on this step.

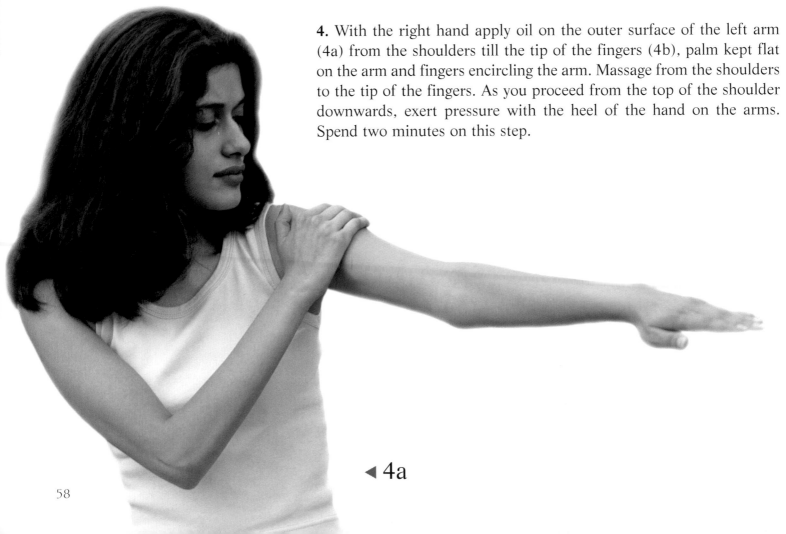

◄ 4a

**5.** After this concentrate on the top of the hand. Place the thumb of the right hand (5a) under the wrist of the left hand. Press the top of the wrist with the remaining fingers of the right hand and massage slowly.

With the palm and fingers of the right hand (5b), circle the top of the hand six to seven times.

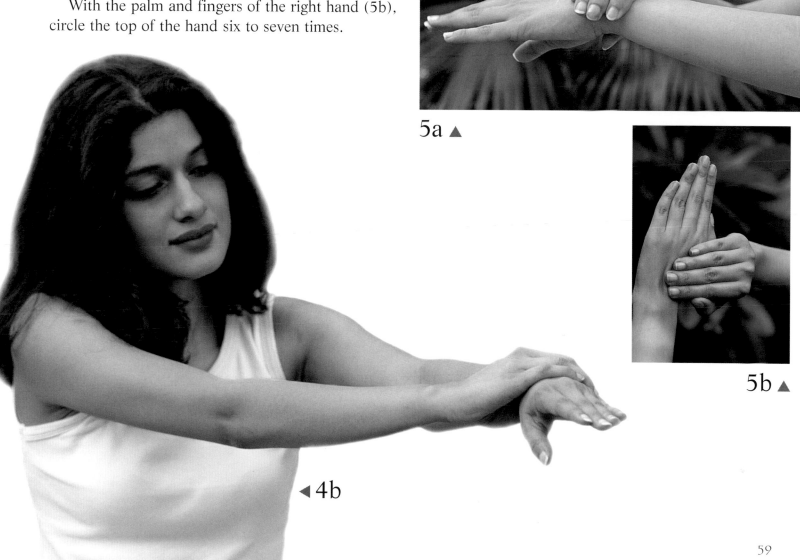

5a ▲

5b ▲

◀ 4b

◄ 6a

**6.** Massage all the fingers, one by one, from the thumb to the little finger. Massage each finger separately with the thumb and index finger, going from the base of the finger to the tip. Keep on varying the pressure and the speed (6a). Pull each finger at a time (6b). This gives the fingers a good stretch and loosens up the knots in the joints of the fingers.

◄ 6b

8 ▲

**7.** Now massage the inner portion of the arms from the armpit. Raise the left arm and with the right hand, do a circular massage into the armpit with the palm and the fingers. Proceed down the arm to the palm and the inner side of the fingers. Keep doing this massage for two minutes.

**8.** Massage the palm in a circular manner along with the fingers. Massage the right hand similarly with the left hand.

7 ▲

**9**. Massage the fingers of both the hands by interlacing them and moving them upwards and downwards.

**10.** From the arms move to the chest. Spread some oil over the chest. With the palm and fingers of the right hand, massage the left region of the chest for two to three minutes exerting comfortable pressure with the palm and stretching the chest outwards. Then massage the right side of the chest with the left hand in the same manner.

**11.** For the upper back region, put your right hand over your left shoulder and effleurage (massage with a circular movement) the spine upwards to the shoulder. Effleurage is done to spread the oil evenly all over the area and make the body relaxed. Massage the back from the spine to the shoulders with your palm and fingers, keeping the pressure. Similarly, with the left hand massage the right side of the back. This also helps the muscles to stretch.

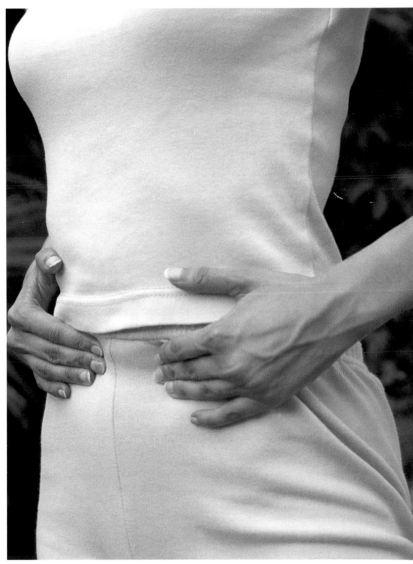

**12.** Now with both your hands massage the abdomen. Keep the palms flat on the abdomen with fingers pointing downwards. Massage the whole of the upper abdomen in a circular manner, pressing to the maximum to loosen up all the fat deposited there. This is the best way to keep the abdomen flat, if done every day. Moreover this massage also helps the bowel movements.

**13.** The lower portion of the abdomen should be tackled next. With both hands kept flat, each pointing towards each other, massage sideways from the centre outwards.

◄ 14

**14.** Now proceed to the lower back region. Place both your hands on the spinal cord with four fingers of both hands touching each other. Exerting pressure, start from the upper part of the lower back and move downwards. Do this ten times. This not only exercises the arms but also provides excellent relief to the backbone.

**15.** Going down to the sacrum, massage with the palms flat, starting with the right hand first and then the left hand.

15 ▼

▲16

17. Now proceed to the buttocks. Well-rounded and firm buttocks can really enhance one's figure, so never allow fat and waste to be stored in this region. Place your left palm just below the hip region. Press it downwards and circle the buttock. Do this massage ten times, and then do the same with the right buttock and the right hand. This activates the area and enhances the muscle tone, thus assisting in detoxification.

17 ▼

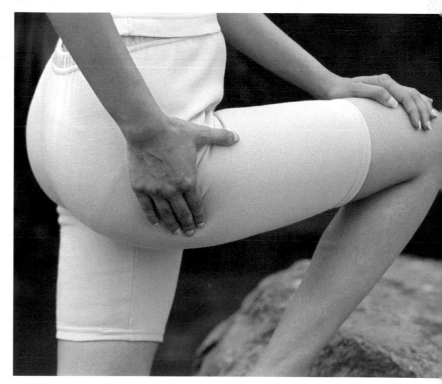

16. Following the curve of the hip, massage the right hip with the right hand first and then the left hip with the left hand. Using pressure, keep the fingers in front and the thumb at the back and massage up and down. The hips are an area where fat tends to stockpile very easily, especially due to a sedentary lifestyle and overeating, accompanied by poor circulation. Massaging of the hips should be done for a little longer time than the rest of the body. Massaging here increases the circulation and helps to break down the fat. It helps the movements of the hip joints by dispensing the toxins.

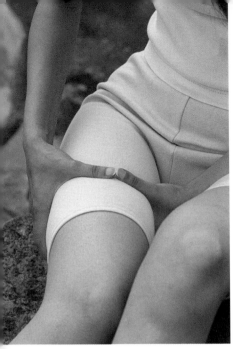  

18 ▲                              19 ▲                              20 ▲

**18.** The thigh muscles are bulky and support the body weight. Kneading brings flexibility to the muscles in the thighs, increasing the blood supply in this region and increasing the exchange of tissue fluids. Place both your hands flat on your thigh, with both thumbs pointing at each other and the four fingers of each hand clasping the thigh at the same position. Applying pressure, move the hands from the top of the thigh downwards till the knee. This massage should be done very firmly, using maximum pressure—in fact, almost sinking the heels of the hands into the muscles. The top of the thigh and the inner region of the thigh are taken care of simultaneously. The right thigh is massaged ten times with both the hands and then the left thigh.

**19.** Using your fingers, palm and heel of the hand, clasp behind the knee firmly, and use the fingers, palm and heel of the other hand to make circles on the entire surface of the knee.

**20.** Now place one hand on top of the knee and keep rubbing the inner surface of the knee to and fro briskly with the other hand. Repeat this on the left knee too.

**21.** The lower leg bears a major part of the body weight. Encircle your lower legs with the thumbs and fingers of both hands. Keep pressing and gliding your thumb pads slowly but with pressure from the knee region to the ankles. This provides a lot of relief to the tight spots in the calf area. The deep pressure pushes the tissues towards the bone and helps to break down the waste products in the muscles. First massage the right leg and then the left one.

**22.** For the ankles and feet you can sit on a stool for support and proceed with the massage. Stroke the ankle bones with your finger tips and thumbs sliding in and out. Massaging the ankles keeps them supple.

21 ▶

**23.** Rest your right hand on top of the right foot and the other hand below the sole. Relax and warm the whole foot by stroking from ankle to toe and heel to toe.

**24.** With both the palms cup the heel into your hands and make circular strokes which relax the sole.

24 ▲           25 ▲

**25.** A good amount of tension builds up in the toes. Massaging every day ensures a release of tension. Hold the foot with one hand and pull each toe from base to tip between your thumb and forefinger, pressing along as you reach the tips and stroking them.

A complete body massage takes almost about half an hour to complete. The body begins to perspire. The skin is the body's main organ of elimination. Wastes, if not disposed of via circulation or as a by-product of the digestive system, are excreted via the skin.

The oil massage must be followed by a warm bath, including shampooing of the hair with cold water. Starting each day in such a manner makes every day unique and precious. ■

# HERBS AND HERBAL OILS—THE 'ROOT'
## OF THE MASSAGE

※

In Ayurveda all the massages—therapeutic and others—are done with herbal oils. These oils are made from herbs whose roots, bark, leaves and flowers have healing properties. Even for self-massage, it is very beneficial to use Ayurvedic herbal oil. Apart from being a medium, oil is also a carrier. While undergoing a massage, some of the medicinal values of the herbal oil are absorbed by the body through its pores. The pores open up due to the heat produced by the massage and the skin absorbs the oil. The oil then enters the bloodstream where it helps the body in its metabolism. Moreover, the oil forms a layer on the skin, protecting it from the heat and dust of the environment.

Oils give the skin a glow and prevent wrinkles and dryness. The oil which used in 90 per cent of the cases is gingelly oil. Coconut oil, castor oil and *ghee* (clarified butter) are used in certain other cases. Gingelly oil suits most constitutions and contains a lot of medicinal properties.

Some of the oils prepared for the head are Sudhabala, Malatyadi, Brahmi and Triphaladi.

Selecting an oil depends on the person's body constitution. The physician decides which oil is suitable for the purpose.

There are oils which promote hair growth, protect the scalp from skin ailments, prevent dandruff, hair loss and premature greying. They make the hair healthy and lustrous and provide comfort to the eyes. They can be used by people of all age groups.

Ayurvedic facial oils provide nourishment to the skin. They also prevent wrinkles and aging, help in the removal of acne, while providing a youthful glowing complexion.

There are more than 1000 formulations for body massage oils. These medicated herbal oils are formulated as per the body constitution, age, nature and symptoms of ailments, and prevalent climatic conditions.

## ▼ Indian Aloe
### *Aloe vera*

DESCRIPTION: This plant is cultivated throughout India and grows wild in the coastal regions. Its leaves are mostly used for medicinal purposes.

USES: A decoction of the plant is prepared and used effectively for general debility, asthma, piles and epilepsy. It is used in the preparation of hair oils for improving hair growth and giving colour to the hair.

## ◄ Indian Beech
### *Pangamia glabra*

DESCRIPTION: This tree is common all over India, from the central Himalayas to southern India and Sri Lanka.

USES: The stems, leaves, fruits, roots and the oil from the seeds of this plant are used. Oil is applied to cure skin diseases, scabies, sores, herpes and eczema. Internally the oil has sometimes been used as a stomachic in cases of dyspepsia with a sluggish liver. A decoction of the leaves is applied during a bath or during fomentation of rheumatic joints. The leaves are also used to cure diarrhoea and coughs.

## ▼ Turmeric
### *Curcuma longa*

DESCRIPTION: Extensively cultivated all over India, the plant's rhizome is dried, powdered and used in cooking to give colour.

USES: Ointments, oils and lotions are prepared from the plant. The juice of the fresh rhizome is used for healing wounds, bruises and leech bites. A paste is made and applied to sprains, wounds and inflamed joints. It is very effective in the case of eczema, prevents skin eruptions and is also a popular remedy for colds. The rhizome, boiled with milk, is given to patients suffering from jaundice.

## ▲ Malabar Nut
### *Adhatoda vasica*

DESCRIPTION: This plant is a bush and grows in most parts of India. Essential oils are prepared from this plant.

USES: Its leaves, roots, flowers and bark have medicinal qualities. It acts as an expectorant, diuretic, antispasmodic. The juice of the fresh leaves taken along with honey is an excellent cough mixture and is useful in curing chronic bronchitis and asthma. The leaves are also used in poultices for massaging rheumatic joints and inflammations.

73

## ◀ Butterfly Pea
### *Clitoria ternatea*

DESCRIPTION: This is a very common garden plant found especially in south India.

USES: Its bark, roots and seeds are used. The seeds contain oil which has a powerful cathartic action. It is used in treating weak eyesight, tumours, colic and constipation. It is also given to remove phlegm in chronic bronchitis.

## ▼ Horse Radish (Drumstick)
### *Moringa oleifera*

Description: It is commonly cultivated in India. Its leaves, flowers, fruit are eaten as vegetables.

Uses: It is very good for inflammatory swellings, gout, acute rheumatism and palsy. Poultices are made from the leaves and used for massage. Decoctions can be made from the leaves and the flowers— these are effective for liver disorders.

## ▶ Tamarind
### *Tamarindus indica*

DESCRIPTION: This is an evergreen tree, cultivated throughout India. The pulp of the fruit, leaves, flowers and bark are used. This fruit is largely used in India for cooking.

USES: The leaves and seeds are astringent; the tender leaves and flowers are cooling and antibilious. The ripe fruit is very good for treating constipation since it acts as a laxative. It is also useful in preventing and curing scurvy. Poultices of the leaves are made and used for treating inflammation of the ankles and joints so that pain is relieved and swelling reduced. The seeds are used for treating diarrhoea and dysentery. Gargling with warm tamarind water relieves a sore throat.

## ▼ Pomegranate
### *Punica granatum*

DESCRIPTION: This fruit is cultivated all over India. The flowers and bark of the tree and the rind of the fruit are astringent and stomachic in quality.

USES: The fruit is beneficial for those convalescing after diarrhoea. The rind is given to people in an advanced stage of dysentry.

## ▼ Asparagus
### *Asparagus recemosus*

DESCRIPTION: This is a climber and is found all over India.

USES: Its root is mostly used as a diuretic, anti-dysentric and as an aphrodisiac. Oils from this climber are used to cure rheumatism, diseases of the joints, stiff neck, hemiplegia and other diseases of the nervous system.

## ▲ Castor Oil Plant
### *Ricinus communis*

DESCRIPTION: This is a perennial bush, commonly found throughout India. The roots, leaves and seeds of this plant are used. Oil is extracted from its seeds.

USES: The leaves of this plant produce oils which are used for massage. The oils are also used for purgation. Decoctions are made from the roots, which are also used as herbal enemas. The plant is used to cure various nervous diseases like lumbago, sciatica, rheumatic swellings and gout.

## ► Holy Basil
### *Ocimum sanctum*

DESCRIPTION: This is a small herb and is found throughout India. Known also as Vermituges, Hindus use it in their religious ceremonics. The leaves, seeds and roots of this herb are used for medicinal purposes. An aromatic plant, it drives away mosquitoes.

USES: It is an excellent expectorant and, therefore, useful in coughs and chest infections. Persons suffering from skin diseases should apply the paste of these leaves on the affected areas.

## ◄ Arjuna Myrobalan
### *Terminalia arjuna*

DESCRIPTION: This is found in the central and southern parts of India.

USES: The bark is an astringent. A decoction for a cardiac stimulant is made from it and is used in the treatment of all types of heart diseases and dropsy. It can also be used as a heart tonic. Its leaves are very useful in curing acne.

# IMPORTANCE OF DIET

Food is essential to keep the body healthy and energetic. Oil massages provide external nutrition to the body and help in preventing diseases, whereas a good diet provides internal nutrition and is necessary for preventing diseases. It is also recommended for growth, development and guarding against wear and tear of the body. A balanced diet is one that contains vitamins, minerals, fibre, fats, carbohydrates, proteins and, of course, water too.

In Ayurveda, foods are classified according to their taste: sweet, sour, salty, pungent, bitter and astringent. The daily food that we eat can be called 'balanced' if all these six tastes are present in our diet. For a healthy person this can be present in varying proportions, depending on the body's demand.

Some sweet-tasting foods are fruit juices, jaggery, sugarcane juice, honey, rice, wheat, milk, corn, soya, cereals, butter, apples, melons, fresh figs, cream, cherries, cardamoms, papayas, raisins.

Some sour-tasting foods are yoghurt, cheese, peaches, pineapples, plums, grapes, lemons, oranges, tamarind, vinegar and tomatoes.

Examples of salty foods are salted nuts, fish, shrimps and pickles.

Some pungent foods are onion, garlic, ginger, radish, asafoetida, mustard and sesame.

Examples of bitter-tasting foods are bitter gourd, leafy vegetables and fenugreek.

Pomegranates, lentils, potatoes, spinach, lettuce, cabbage, cauliflower, celery and nutmeg are some astringent foods. Herbs and spices such as cardamom, cinnamon, turmeric, black pepper, cummin, coriander, chilli are not only added to food for taste, but are important for health.

A person's biological make-up like his age is taken into consideration while deciding on an ideal diet: a child's diet should not be the same as that of a young man, just as the diet would vary in old age too. Another factor taken into consideration is the seasons: seasonal vegetables and fruits should be consumed as they will be available fresh and the nutritional value of the food will be richest during the season. Keeping this in view it is important that each person should be eating easy-to-digest and nutritious food. The food should be hot and freshly cooked; it should be tasty and the proper amount should be taken.

A meal should be taken only after the previous meal has been properly digested. Food should be eaten amidst pleasant and clear surroundings and a meal should not be rushed through. It is important that the quality of the food be good. Processed and canned food should be avoided.

There should be a discipline in eating; regular meal times ought to be maintained for proper digestion. Breakfast should be eaten before 8 a.m. and should be light, while dinner time should ideally be before 9 p.m. The afternoon meal should be substantial for this is the time when the body's digestive power is at its highest and food is digested well. Dinner should be lighter than lunch since the digestive ability slows down towards the evening—it should be over two hours before bedtime.

In between lunch and dinner, if your body feels the need for intake of food, then a small evening snack could be taken to maintain the energy level in the body.

Drinking plenty of water with every meal is essential to stimulate digestion. The water should be warm or of room temperature. Improper nutrition is almost always the cause of physical illness. You should concentrate on food that helps the body to operate more smoothly rather than adding to its burden by eating a non-vegetarian diet.

An adult's daily food should normally comprise the following:

Fruits, fruit juice, rice, *chappatis*, bread, cooked vegetables, steamed vegetables, cooked pulses and milk in the proportion of 40-60% of whole grains, 10-20% of high quality proteins and 30-50% of fresh fruits and vegetables. This is good for all healthy persons. If you are suffering from any disease, special herbal medicines, specific Ayurvedic oils and certain foods are recommended and a certain routine has to be followed.

Only three-fourths of the stomach should be filled with food; the rest should be partly filled with water and some space should be left for digestion.

Another important aspect is the disposal of waste products generated from the consumption of food. However nutritious be the food that is eaten, if proper digestion does not take place, and waste is not expelled from the system, the food is converted into toxins.

Hence when the body is in balance, the body's intuitive sense will guide us towards a proper Ayurvedic diet. ∎

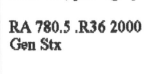

## The Goodness in Foods

| FOOD GROUP | MAIN NUTRIENTS | FOOD GROUP | MAIN NUTRIENTS |
|---|---|---|---|
| **CEREALS: GRAINS AND PRODUCTS**<br>Rice, Wheat, Millet, Maize, Milo, Barley, Rice flakes, Wheat Flour | Energy, Protein, Invisible fat, Vitamin-B1, Vitamin-B2, Folic acid, Iron, Fibre | **VEGETABLES (GREEN LEAFY)**<br>Amaranth, Spinach, Drumstick leaves, Coriander leaves, Mustard leaves, Fenugreek leaves | Invisible fats, Carotenoids, Vitamin-B2, Folic acid Calcium, Iron, Fibre |
| **PULSES AND LEGUMES**<br>Bengal gram, Black gram, Green gram, Red gram, Lentils (whole as well as split), Cow peas, Peas, Kidney beans, Soya beans, Beans, etc. | Energy, Protein, Invisible fat, Vitamin-B1, Vitamin-B2, Folic acid, Calcium, Iron, Fibre | **OTHER VEGETABLES**<br>Carrots, Brinjals, Ladies' fingers, Capsicums, Beans, Onions, Drumsticks, Cauliflower | Carotenoids, Folic acid, Calcium, Fibre |
| **MILK PRODUCTS**<br>Milk, Curd, Skimmed milk, Cheese | Protein, Fat, Vitamin-B2, Calcium | **FATS**<br>Butter, *Ghee* (Clarified butter), Hydrogenated oils, Cooking oils like Ground nut, Mustard, Coconut | Energy, Fat, Essential fatty acids |
| **MEAT PRODUCTS**<br>Chicken, Liver, Fish, Egg, Meat | Protein, Fat, Vitamin-B2 | **SUGARS**<br>Sugar, Jaggery | Energy |
| **FRUITS**<br>Mangoes, Guavas, Ripe tomatoes, Papayas, Oranges, Sweet limes, Water melons | Carotenoids, Vitamin-C, Fibre | | |

*Source:* National Institute of Nutrition, Hyderabad, India.

# APPENDIX

## Names of Herbs and Plants in Different Languages

| English | Botanical | Sanskrit | Hindi | Malayalam |
|---|---|---|---|---|
| Indian Aloe | *Aloe vera* | Ghrita-Kumari | Ghikanvara/Kumari | Kattarvazha |
| Indian Beech | *Pangamia glabra* | — | — | — |
| Turmeric | *Curcuma longa* | Rajani/Haridra | Haldi | Manjal |
| Malabar Nut | *Adhatoda vasica* | Vasaka | Adoosa | Adalodakam |
| Castor Oil plant | *Ricinus communis* | — | Erandi | Avanakku |
| Arjuna Myrobalan | *Terminalia arjuna* | Arjuna | Arjun/Kahu | Maruthu |
| Tamarind | *Tamarindus indica* | Tintrini | Imli | Puli |
| Pomegranate | *Punica granatum* | Dadimam | Mathala Pazham | Anar |
| Asparagus | *Asparagus recemosus* | Satavari | Satavar | Satavari |
| Horse Radish (Drumstick) | *Moringa oleifera* | Sigru | Sahinjan | Muringa |
| Holy Basil | *Ocimum sanctum* | Tulasi/Divya | Tulasi | Tulasi |
| Butterfly Pea | *Clitoria ternatea* | Aparajita | Aparajita | Sankha Pushpam |
| Margosa tree | *Melia azadirachta* | Nimba | Neem | Veppu |
| Gigantic Swallow Wort (Mudar) | *Calatropis gigantea* | Arka | Ak | Erukka |
| Indian Penny Wort | *Hydrocotyle asiatica* | Brahmi | Brahmi/Khulakudi | Brahmi |
| Hibiscus | *Hibiscus rosasinensis* | Japa/Rudra Pushpa | Gudhal/Jasund | Chemparuthi |

# The Goodness in Foods

| FOOD GROUP | MAIN NUTRIENTS |
|---|---|
| **CEREALS: GRAINS AND PRODUCTS** Rice, Wheat, Millet, Maize, Milo, Barley, Rice flakes, Wheat Flour | Energy, Protein, Invisible fat, Vitamin-B1, Vitamin-B2, Folic acid, Iron, Fibre |
| **PULSES AND LEGUMES** Bengal gram, Black gram, Green gram, Red gram, Lentils (whole as well as split), Cow peas, Peas, Kidney beans, Soya beans, Beans, etc. | Energy, Protein, Invisible fat, Vitamin-B1, Vitamin-B2, Folic acid, Calcium, Iron, Fibre |
| **MILK PRODUCTS** Milk, Curd, Skimmed milk, Cheese | Protein, Fat, Vitamin-B2, Calcium |
| **MEAT PRODUCTS** Chicken, Liver, Fish, Egg, Meat | Protein, Fat, Vitamin-B2 |
| **FRUITS** Mangoes, Guavas, Ripe tomatoes, Papayas, Oranges, Sweet limes, Water melons | Carotenoids, Vitamin-C, Fibre |

| FOOD GROUP | MAIN NUTRIENTS |
|---|---|
| **VEGETABLES (GREEN LEAFY)** Amaranth, Spinach, Drumstick leaves, Coriander leaves, Mustard leaves, Fenugreek leaves | Invisible fats, Carotenoids, Vitamin-B2, Folic acid Calcium, Iron, Fibre |
| **OTHER VEGETABLES** Carrots, Brinjals, Ladies' fingers, Capsicums, Beans, Onions, Drumsticks, Cauliflower | Carotenoids, Folic acid, Calcium, Fibre |
| **FATS** Butter, *Ghee* (Clarified butter), Hydrogenated oils, Cooking oils like Ground nut, Mustard, Coconut | Energy, Fat, Essential fatty acids |
| **SUGARS** Sugar, Jaggery | Energy |

*Source:* National Institute of Nutrition, Hyderabad, India.

# APPENDIX

## Names of Herbs and Plants in Different Languages

| English | Botanical | Sanskrit | Hindi | Malayalam |
|---|---|---|---|---|
| Indian Aloe | *Aloe vera* | Ghrita-Kumari | Ghikanvara/Kumari | Kattarvazha |
| Indian Beech | *Pangamia glabra* | — | — | — |
| Turmeric | *Curcuma longa* | Rajani/Haridra | Haldi | Manjal |
| Malabar Nut | *Adhatoda vasica* | Vasaka | Adoosa | Adalodakam |
| Castor Oil plant | *Ricinus communis* | — | Erandi | Avanakku |
| Arjuna Myrobalan | *Terminalia arjuna* | Arjuna | Arjun/Kahu | Maruthu |
| Tamarind | *Tamarindus indica* | Tintrini | Imli | Puli |
| Pomegranate | *Punica granatum* | Dadimam | Mathala Pazham | Anar |
| Asparagus | *Asparagus recemosus* | Satavari | Satavar | Satavari |
| Horse Radish (Drumstick) | *Moringa oleifera* | Sigru | Sahinjan | Muringa |
| Holy Basil | *Ocimum sanctum* | Tulasi/Divya | Tulasi | Tulasi |
| Butterfly Pea | *Clitoria ternatea* | Aparajita | Aparajita | Sankha Pushpam |
| Margosa tree | *Melia azadirachta* | Nimba | Neem | Veppu |
| Gigantic Swallow Wort (Mudar) | *Calatropis gigantea* | Arka | Ak | Erukka |
| Indian Penny Wort | *Hydrocotyle asiatica* | Brahmi | Brahmi/Khulakudi | Brahmi |
| Hibiscus | *Hibiscus rosasinensis* | Japa/Rudra Pushpa | Gudhal/Jasund | Chemparuthi |